PRACTICE
MATH

BOOK 4

SKILL REVIEW FOR HOME AND SCHOOL

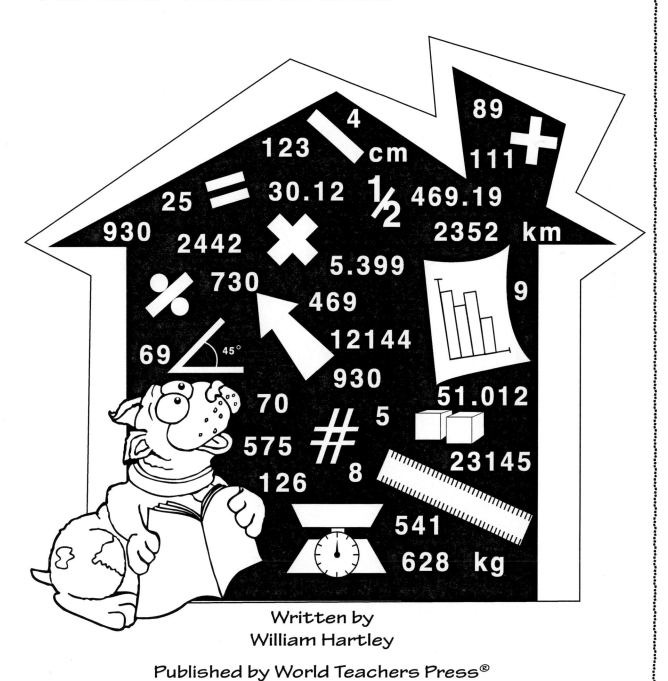

Written by
William Hartley

Published by World Teachers Press®

Order Number 2-5133
ISBN 1-58324-057-8

B C D E F 10 09 08 07 06

395 Main Street
Rowley, MA 01969
www.didax.com

Foreword

The *Practice Math: Skill Review for Home and School* series provides you with a useful, relevant and enjoyable way of providing students with mathematics to do at home. The activities in the four books do not require hours of preparation or correction on your part. In fact, by providing parents with a set of answer sheets, even the correcting could be carried out at home where appropriate.

The worksheets are a method of providing mathematics homework for those students who either want it or need it! Their purpose is not to stretch the able or confound the struggling. It is to reinforce and give the students practice at carrying out operations and tasks already taught and mastered in the classroom. Parents should be encouraged to help their children with the worksheets where necessary, however, students should be able to complete the worksheets independently providing the worksheet is within the ability level of the student.

Book 4 has thirty-eight worksheets split into eleven topics each of which forms an important part of the mathematics curriculum. The worksheets in each topic grouping–as outlined in the Contents information below–are individually titled to give a clear indication of their content. A photocopiable Student's Record Sheet for your or parents' use is included on Page 5.

The publisher has chosen to use metric measurements for most activities in this book. The National Council of Teachers of Math supports the use of the metric system as an integral part of the mathematics curriculum at all levels of education (NCTM Position Statement on Metrication, 1986).

In some activities Imperial (English) measurements are used for illustrative purposes.

Contents

Teachers Notes 4

Student's Record Sheet 5

Angles

Supplementary and Complementary 6

Bearings 7

Area

Area Calculations 8

Area Problems 9

Coordinates First the Clue—Then the Answer 10

Moving Round Town 11

Data

Return Journeys 12

Pie Charts 13

Information Interpretation! 14

Length

Units of Length 15

Scale Drawing 16

Money

Addition and Subtraction of Money 17

Supermarket Shopping 18

Multiplication and Division of Money ... 19

Number

Addition of Whole Numbers 20

Addition of Fractions 21

Subtraction of Fractions 22

Subtraction of Whole Numbers 23

Number

Multiplication of Fractions 24

Division of Fractions 25

Decimal Addition 26

Decimal Subtraction 27

Multiplication of Whole Numbers 28

Decimal Multiplication 29

Decimal Division 30

Division of Whole Numbers 31

Averages 32

Four Rules Problems 33

Crossnumbers 34

Probability From Certainty to Impossibility 35

What Are Your Chances of...? 36

Time

Only a Matter of Time! 37

Before, After and Between 38

Volume and Capacity

Volume Calculations 39

Capacity Calculations 40

Volume and Capacity Problems 41

Weight

Right or Wrong 42

Weighty Problems! 43

Answers .... 44—48

Teachers Notes

The *Practice Math: Skill Review for Home and School* series provides you with a resource that has multiple uses within the classroom and at home. These include:

1. Use as review activities. As each worksheet focuses on one specific math concept, the worksheets can be used as a whole-class resource to review and consolidate class work.

2. Use as individual remediation resources. When focusing on individual needs the sheets can be used to re-teach concepts that students have struggled to master.

3. Use as extension. The worksheets are ideal for use by those students who have achieved mastery of a concept earlier than the majority of the class.

4. Use as specific homework activities. By using the worksheets, you will be able to send home work that relates specifically to what is being taught in the class at that time.

5. Use as partner work. The worksheets are an ideal resource for peer interaction and tutoring.

Features of the Worksheets

1. General area of math identified

2. Specific concepts identified

3. Diagrammatic representation used wherever possible

4. Space to record progress

5. Basic background to the concept developed is provided to assist both student and parent.

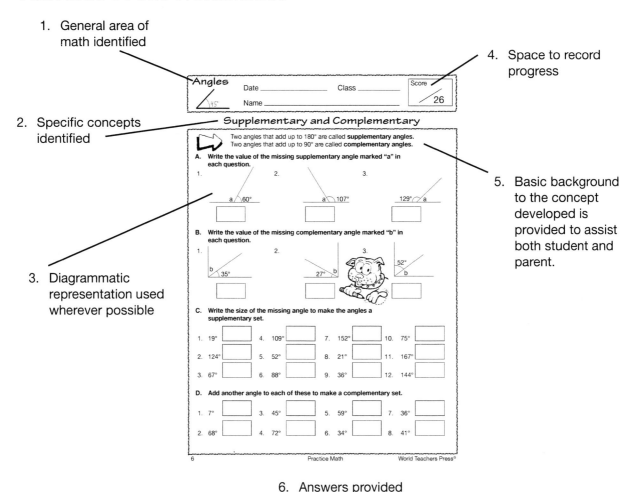

6. Answers provided

How well have I done?

Name: _____   Class: _____

Group	Page No.	Worksheet Title	Date	Score	Total
Angles	6	Supplementary and Complementary			26
	7	Bearings			22
Area	8	Area Calculations			27
	9	Area Problems			10
Coordinates	10	First the Clue — Then the Answer			3
	11	Moving Round Town			13
Data	12	Return Journeys			8
	13	Pie Charts			12
	14	Information Interpretation!			3
Length	15	Units of Length			24
	16	Scale Drawing			24
Money	17	Addition and Subtraction of Money			37
	18	Supermarket Shopping			10
	19	Multiplication and Division of Money			37
Number	20	Addition of Whole Numbers			24
	21	Addition of Fractions			30
	22	Subtraction of Fractions			30
	23	Subtraction of Whole Numbers			36
	24	Multiplication of Fractions			30
	25	Division of Fractions			30
	26	Decimal Addition			28
	27	Decimal Subtraction			27
	28	Multiplication of Whole Numbers			36
	29	Decimal Multiplication			36
	30	Decimal Division			26
	31	Division of Whole Numbers			36
	32	Averages			12
	33	Four Rules Problems			13
	34	Crossnumbers			19
Probability	35	From Certainty to Impossibility			6
	36	What Are Your Chances of...?			18
Time	37	Only a Matter of Time!			11
	38	Before, After and Between			24
Volume and Capacity	39	Volume Calculations			16
	40	Capacity Calculations			24
	41	Volume and Capacity Problems			12
Weight	42	Right or Wrong			28
	43	Weighty Problems!			13

Name _____

Date _____   Class _____

Score

/ 26

Supplementary and Complementary

Two angles that add up to 180° are called **supplementary angles.**
Two angles that add up to 90° are called **complementary angles.**

A. Write the value of the missing supplementary angle marked "a" in each question.

1. 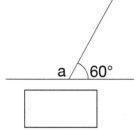 a / 60°

[ ]

2. a \ 107°

[ ]

3. 129° \ a

[ ]

B. Write the value of the missing complementary angle marked "b" in each question.

1. 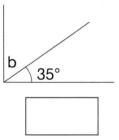 b 35°

[ ]

2. 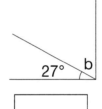 27° b

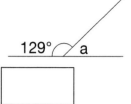 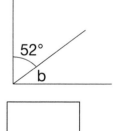

[ ]

3. 52° b

[ ]

C. Write the size of the missing angle to make the angles a supplementary set.

1. 19° [ ]
2. 124° [ ]
3. 67° [ ]

4. 109° [ ]
5. 52° [ ]
6. 88° [ ]

7. 152° [ ]
8. 21° [ ]
9. 36° [ ]

10. 75° [ ]
11. 167° [ ]
12. 144° [ ]

D. Add another angle to each of these to make a complementary set.

1. 7° [ ]
2. 68° [ ]

3. 45° [ ]
4. 72° [ ]

5. 59° [ ]
6. 34° [ ]

7. 36° [ ]
8. 41° [ ]

Name _____

Date _____ Class _____

Score

/22

Bearings

A bearing gives the direction from one place to another. The bearing of an object is the angle measured clockwise from north to the object. A bearing is always written using three digits.

So, 9° would be written 009° and 240° would be written 240°.

Bearing = 009°

 351°

A. Using the information above, write the following angles as bearings.

1. 6° [   ]   3. 74° [   ]   5. 126° [   ]   7. 53° [   ]

2. 320° [   ]   4. 28° [   ]   6. 2° [   ]   8. 247° [   ]

B. Write the following bearings as angles.

1. 002° [   ]   3. 142° [   ]   5. 099° [   ]   7. 023° [   ]

2. 035° [   ]   4. 017° [   ]   6. 071° [   ]   8. 086° [   ]

C. In each of the questions below write the bearing traveling from A to B.

You do not need to actually measure the angle. A simple subtraction problem will give you the answer.

1.
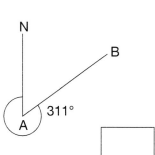

3.
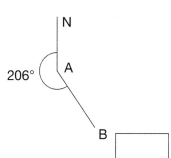

5.
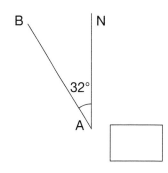

2.
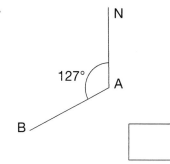

4.
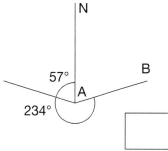

6.
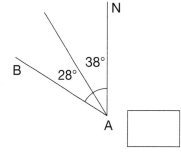

Name _____

Date _____ Class _____

Score

/ 27

Area Calculations

Area is the amount of surface covered by a shape. It is measured in square units. Square millimeters (mm^2), square centimeters (cm^2), square meters (m^2) and square kilometers (km^2) are commonly used square units. To find the area of a rectangular plane shape, multiply the length by the width. Remember that 100 mm^2 = 1 cm^2.

A.   Find the area of the following shapes in cm^2.

1. 43 cm x 26 cm = _____   4. 15 cm x 83 cm = _____   7. 94 cm x 81 cm = _____

2. 25 cm x 67 cm = _____   5. 97 cm x 46 cm = _____   8. 27 cm x 75 cm = _____

3. 23 cm x 68 cm = _____   6. 54 cm x 82 cm = _____   9. 90 cm x 90 cm = _____

B.   Now find the area of these shapes in m^2.

1.   36 m x 6 m = _____   3.   64 m x 8 m = _____   5.   57 m x 11 m = _____

2.   12 m x 28 m = _____   4.   85 m x 15 m = _____   6.   9 m x 79 m = _____

C.   Measure and calculate the area of each of these shapes in mm^2.
Then find the total area of all the shapes.
Record the final answer in cm^2.

A	B	C	D	E

Final answer [   ] cm^2

D.   Finally, figure out the area of these shapes in km^2.

1. 56 km x 14 km = _____   3. 22 km x 37 km = _____   5. 48 km x 56 km = _____

2. 29 km x 93 km = _____   4. 75 km x 62 km= _____   6. 73 km x 89 km = _____

Area

Name _____

Date _____ Class _____

Score

/ 10

Area Problems

The area of a rectangular shape equals length x width. Remember this when completing the problems on this sheet. You might find graph paper useful while completing the questions and checking your answers.

Answer these questions.

1. A rectangle measures 16 m long and 50 cm wide. What is its area in m^2?

2. By how much is an area of 3,256 km^2 less than an area of 7,389 km^2?

3. A box of chocolates is 20 cm long and 8 cm wide.
   What is the total area of the top and the bottom of the box?

4. The area of a rectangular driveway is 150 m^2. It is 3 m wide.
   What is its length in meters?

5. What is the total surface area of a rectangular prism measuring
   3 cm x 7 cm x 5 cm?

6. How many times greater is an area of 12 m x 14 m than an area 6 m x 7 m?

7. If half of a carpet measuring 9 m x 6 m is placed next to half of a
   carpet measuring 12 m x 8 m, what area of floor would be covered?

8. A square porcelain tile has an area of 900 cm^2.
   What is the length of one side?

9. A piece of paper is 10 cm wide and 24 cm long.
   A 2-cm strip is cut from its length.
   What area, in cm^2, is the piece of paper now?

10. A plastic sheet is 8 m long and 4 m wide.
    What will its area be if 1 m is cut from all four sides?

Coordinates

Name _____

Date _____   Class _____

Score

/ 3

First the Clue—Then the Answer

Coordinates are an ordered pair of numbers which show a point on a graph, grid or map. The first number is the horizontal coordinate and the second number is the vertical coordinate. If the numbers on the horizontal axis are extended to the left of 0, they are written as negative amounts.

A. The grid contains the letters of a three-word clue to a mathematical shape. In order to find the clue you will have to arrange the letters in the correct order. You can do this by reading their coordinates in the order given below. As you read each coordinate write each letter in the same order in the box provided.

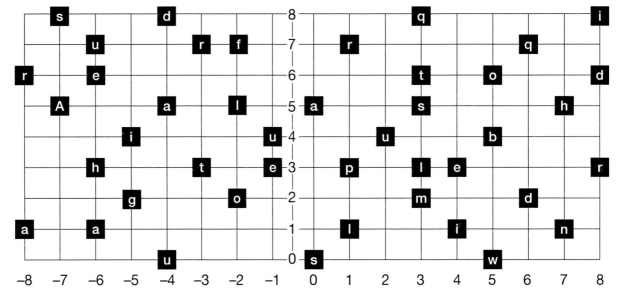

(–7, 5), (7, 1); (-6, 6), (3, 8), (–1, 4), (8, 8), (3, 3), (0, 5), (-3, 3), (4, 3), (1, 7), (–4, 5), (-2, 5);

(1, 3), (-4, 5), (-3, 7), (–6, 1), (3, 3), (-2, 5); (–1, 3), (3, 3), (5, 6), (–5, 2), (-8, 6), (-8, 1), (3, 2)

[ ]

B. What is the answer to the clue? [ ]

C. Read these coordinates in the same way as Section A to either find or check the answer. Write it in the box on the right.

(–3, 7), (–6, 3), (5, 6), (3, 2), (5, 4), (–6, 7), (3, 5)

[ ]

Name _____

Date _____

Class _____

Score ___/ 13

Moving Round Town

Coordinates are an ordered pair of numbers which show a point on a graph, grid or map. The first number is the horizontal coordinate and the second number is the vertical coordinate.

Look at the information shown on the grid. Answer the questions at the bottom of the page.

The compass showing eight points of direction will be useful.

1. Which building is north of the town hall? _____

2. What would you find at the coordinates $9\frac{1}{2}, 2\frac{1}{2}$? _____

3. In which direction from the town hall is the bus station? _____

4. In which direction from the school is the post office? _____

5. Give the coordinates for: (a) the hospital and (b) the train station. (a)_____ (b)_____

6. Which building is east of the hospital? _____

7. The cafe coordinates are: _____

8. The bank coordinates are: _____

9. The bank is _____ of the bus station,

   and _____ of the school.

10. Which two buildings are directly northeast of the cafe?

   _____ and _____

Name _____

Date _____   Class _____

Score

_____ / 8

Return Journeys

A chart is a way of showing information in a clear, easy-to-understand form. Charts are one of the most common ways of displaying data. Distance, cost and time are some of the most frequent details shown on a chart.

The chart below is used by tourists and shows the distance between some of the major towns and cities in Britain. To find the distance between Birmingham and Cardiff, look down the column under the heading Birmingham until you reach the row containing Cardiff. The distance is 108 miles. Use the chart in this way to answer the questions below.

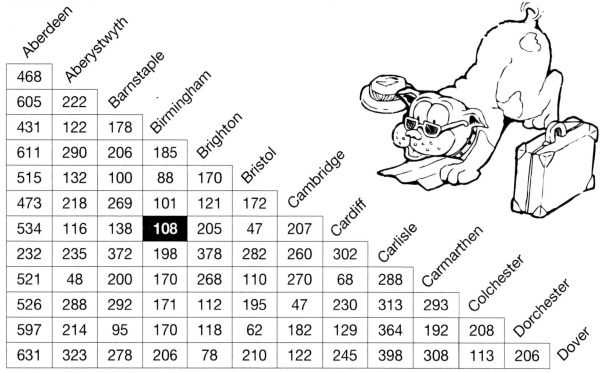

Aberdeen	Aberystwyth	Barnstaple	Birmingham	Brighton	Bristol	Cambridge	Cardiff	Carlisle	Carmarthen	Colchester	Dorchester	Dover
468												
605	222											
431	122	178										
611	290	206	185									
515	132	100	88	170								
473	218	269	101	121	172							
534	116	138	**108**	205	47	207						
232	235	372	198	378	282	260	302					
521	48	200	170	268	110	270	68	288				
526	288	292	171	112	195	47	230	313	293			
597	214	95	170	118	62	182	129	364	192	208		
631	323	278	206	78	210	122	245	398	308	113	206	

A. Write the total distance in miles of eight round trip journeys between the following towns.

1. Cambridge and Aberystwyth _____

2. Aberdeen and Colchester _____

3. Dorchester and Carlisle _____

4. Dover and Brighton _____

5. Bristol and Barnstaple _____

6. Birmingham and Carmarthen _____

B. Now try these problems.

1. Deduct the total of 9 round trip journeys from Cardiff to Barnstaple from the total of 7 round trip journeys from Brighton to Carlisle. _____

2. Multiply the greatest distance shown on the chart by 12 and divide your answer by 6. _____

Name _____   Score

Date _____   Class _____   /12

Pie Charts

A pie chart is a circular diagram divided into fractions and shows how something is divided. The size of each fraction on the chart is worked out using angles. Each completed chart has 360° Remember this when you answer the questions.

A.   Look at the chart. Answer the questions.

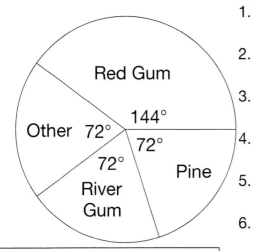

1.   What fraction of the forest has pine trees growing in it?

2.   What percentage of the forest is made up of pine and river gum trees?

3.   Which is the most common tree to be found there?   _____

4.   What fraction of the forest is not made up of red gum trees?

5.   What percentage of the forest is made up of river gum trees?

6.   What percentage of trees is not pine trees?

7.   What angle would be shown on the pie chart to represent a quarter of something?

Number of each tree species found in Bluebell Forest.
Red Gum – 72, Pine – 36
River Gum – 36, Other types – 36

B.   Transfer the information below to the empty pie chart on the right. Mark the angle as well as the car color in each segment. You will need to use a ruler and a protractor.

Number of each car color seen during a traffic survey.
Red – 60, Blue – 40,
Green – 30, Yellow – 10,
Other colors – 60

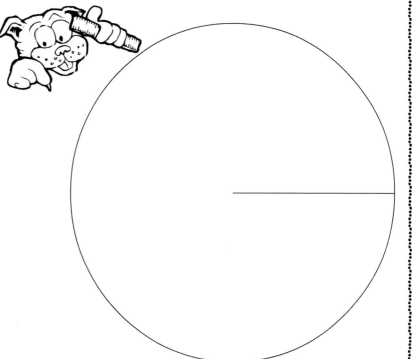

Information Interpretation!

A bar graph uses columns or rows to display data. In a bar graph, the data is displayed using either vertical or horizontal lines. A pie chart is a diagrammatic method of showing data in which the size of a sector of a circle corresponds to the frequency of the set represented.

Box 1 contains information. Read it. Display the information you have just read in the form of a column bar graph in Box 2, a horizontal bar graph in Box 3 and a pie chart in Box 4. Remember to annotate your diagrams and, in the case of the pie chart, write in the angles used for each sector of the chart.

1.

There are 30 students in Grade 6 at North Road School.

In a survey carried out by these students last September, it was discovered that 12 of them walked to school, 10 came by car, 5 rode their bikes and the other 3 came by bus.

3.

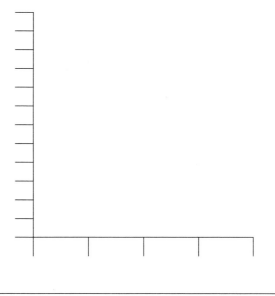

2.

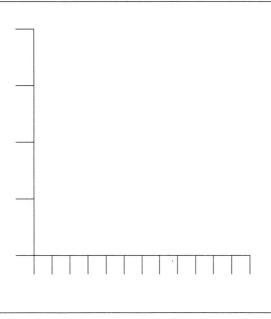

4.

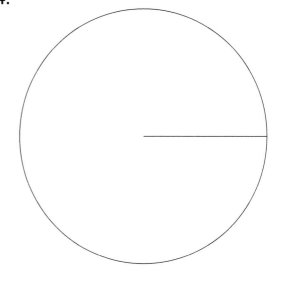

Units of Length

 Very short lengths are measured in millimeters (mm). Short lengths are measured in centimeters (cm). Longer lengths are measured in meters (m). Very long lengths are measured in kilometers (km).

10 mm = 1 cm, 100 cm = 1 m, 1 000 m = 1 km.

When completing these problems use a separate piece of paper to do your work and check your answers on a calculator if you have one.

A. Add the following millimeter amounts and write your answers in centimeters.

1. 147 mm + 160 mm + 113 mm = ☐ cm   4. 650 mm + 459 mm + 841 mm = ☐ cm

2. 980 mm + 997 mm + 943 mm = ☐ cm   5. 379 mm + 927 mm + 834 mm = ☐ cm

3. 704 mm + 980 mm + 626 mm = ☐ cm   6. 684 mm + 897 mm + 989 mm = ☐ cm

B. In this section, multiply your Section A answer by the number shown. Write your results in meters and centimeters.

1. 7 _____   3. 8 _____   5. 9 _____

2. 11 _____   4. 12 _____   6. 15 _____

C. Subtract these centimeter amounts and give your answers in meters and centimeters.

1. 7,959 cm – 4,665 cm = _____   4. 6,200 cm – 4,135 cm = _____

2. 7,007 cm – 6,467 cm = _____   5. 6,775 cm – 4,387 cm = _____

3. 6,000 cm – 4,359 cm = _____   6. 8,436 cm – 6,962 cm = _____

D. In this section, divide your Section C answer by the number shown. Write your result in meters using decimal notation.

1. 9 ☐   4. 7 ☐

2. 6 ☐   5. 4 ☐

3. 3 ☐   6. 2 ☐

Length

Name _____

Date _____ Class _____

Score /24

Scale Drawing

A scale drawing is a drawing on which every measurement is in proportion to the actual or real measurement. For example, if a distance of 5 m is shown on a drawing as a line 5 cm long, the drawing will be at a scale of 1 cm to 1 m. This means that 1 m in real measurement is shown as 1 cm on the drawing. You will need a ruler, a protractor and a sharp pencil.

A. Make labeled scale drawings of these rough sketch plans. Use the scale given for each one.

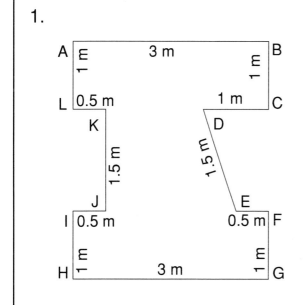

1.

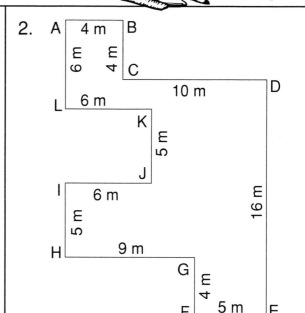

2.

Scale 2 cm:1 m   Scale 1 cm:2 m

Name _____

Score

Date _____ Class _____

/37

Addition and Subtraction of Money

Addition and subtraction problems involving money can be done in columns like any addition and subtraction problems. Before writing the answers on this worksheet, complete your calculations on a separate piece of paper.

A. Complete the table by adding each of the amounts in Column A to each of the amounts in Row A. Don't forget the decimal point to separate dollars and cents.

Addition of Money					
+	$	$	$	$	$
A	13.75	23.48	26.87	37.87	46.49
18.77	32.52				
27.55		51.03			
35.86			62.73		82.35
44.65				82.52	

B. Write the cost of seven items if two are priced at the amounts below.

1. $13.14 [ ]   2. $16.22 [ ]   3. $25.50 [ ]

C. Complete the table by subtracting each of the amounts in Column A from each of the amounts in Row A.

Subtraction of Money					
-	$	$	$	$	$
A	19.79	28.32	47.60	63.12	84.45
10.99	8.80				
12.76					71.69
14.38		13.94		48.74	
17.85			29.75		

D. What will be the change from $20.00 if you bought two items each costing the amounts shown below?

1. $6.49 [ ]   2. $8.26 [ ]   3. $2.72 [ ]   4. $7.84 [ ]

Supermarket Shopping

All the questions below are about the supermarket receipt on the right of the page. Do the problems on a separate piece of paper. You may use a calculator to check your answers.

Give the answer to the questions using the dollar sign where appropriate, ex. $3.25.

1. What was the total cost of the fruit and vegetables?

2. How much more expensive were items 1, 4, 7, 10 and 12 than items 2, 8, 9, 11 and 19?

3. What was the total cost of items 13, 14, 15 and 16?

4. By how much would a 10% discount on items 2, 6 and 19 reduce their total cost?

5. What is the difference in price between the most expensive item and the cheapest one?

6. Which item was 10¢ more than a third of the cost of the jam?

   _____

7. Three of the items on the receipt have a price that is a multiple of 5.

   Which 3 items are they? _____,

   _____ and _____

8. How much would have been paid for all the items listed on this supermarket receipt?

Freshy's Supermarket

Item	Cost
1. Kitchen towels	$1.19
2. Orange juice	$0.51
3. Bananas	$0.79
4. Peaches	$0.92
5. Grapes	$1.48
6. Wholewheat bread	$1.49
7. Rice pudding	$0.98
8. Granulated sugar	$0.75
9. Bleach	$1.09
10. Milk	$1.77
11. Sandwich spread	$0.49
12. Cream	$0.63
13. Roast pork	$4.11
14. Steak	$3.34
15. Cooked turkey	$2.21
16. Cheese	$1.94
17. Soup	$1.42
18. Stir-fry sauce	$1.19
19. Chips	$2.20
20. Jam	$2.46
21. Cucumbers	$0.70

Name _____

Date _____   Class _____

Score _____/ 37

Multiplication and Division of Money

These questions require multiplication or division to find the answers. Complete your calculations on a separate piece of paper before writing your results on the sheet.

A. Complete the table by multiplying each of the amounts in Row A by each of the numbers in Column A.
Don't forget to write a decimal point to separate dollars and cents.

Multiplication of Money					
×	$	$	$	$	$
A	2.19	3.82	5.37	8.64	10.95
6	13.14				
7		26.74			
8			42.96		87.60
9				77.76	

B. Multiply the amount in number 1 by 9, number 2 by 11 and number three by 12.

1. $16.48 [____]   2. $24.36 [____]   3. $37.12 [____]

C. Complete the table by dividing each of the amounts in Row A by each of the numbers in Column A.

Division of Money					
÷	$	$	$	$	$
A	121.92	129.60	123.84	1,211.52	125.76
6	20.32				
2					62.88
4		32.40		302.88	
3			41.28		

D. Find $\frac{2}{3}$ of the amounts shown in numbers 1 and 2 and $\frac{3}{5}$ of the amounts in numbers 3 and 4.

1. $8.34 [____]   2. $9.84 [____]   3. $6.75 [____]   4. $9.95 [____]

Number

Name _____

Date _____ Class _____

Score ____/24

Addition of Whole Numbers

➡ Here are some addition problems. Before writing the answers, you should do the problems on a separate piece of paper. If you have a calculator, you can use it to check your answers.

A.   These problems are easy. They only have carrying from the ones.

1. $3,229 + 1,329 + 1,429 =$ ⬚

2. $4,139 + 1,126 + 4,514 =$ ⬚

3. $2,229 + 4,253 + 2,304 =$ ⬚

4. $2,226 + 1,312 + 1,333 =$ ⬚

5. $4,316 + 4,216 + 1,237 =$ ⬚

6. $1,007 + 2,249 + 2,005 =$ ⬚

B.   These problems are slightly harder. They have carrying from the ones and tens.

1. $2,235 + 1,199 + 5,387 =$ ⬚

2. $1,189 + 1,192 + 1,279 =$ ⬚

3. $2,174 + 1,526 + 4,251 =$ ⬚

4. $1,109 + 1,146 + 3,475 =$ ⬚

5. $1,344 + 6,058 + 1,192 =$ ⬚

6. $1,497 + 1,163 + 5,261 =$ ⬚

C.   These problems are harder still! They have carrying from three columns.

1. $3,883 + 1,924 + 3,569 =$ ⬚

2. $1,697 + 5,505 + 1,999 =$ ⬚

3. $1,088 + 4,998 + 2,999 =$ ⬚

4. $1,587 + 4,079 + 2,693 =$ ⬚

5. $4,496 + 3,885 + 1,434 =$ ⬚

6. $1,596 + 2,899 + 4,906 =$ ⬚

D.   These problems are the hardest of all! They have carrying from all four columns.

1. $5,964 + 6,740 + 9,728 =$ ⬚

2. $3,899 + 9,786 + 8,155 =$ ⬚

3. $9,467 + 6,757 + 7,559 =$ ⬚

4. $9,399 + 7,725 + 6,051 =$ ⬚

5. $9,695 + 9,378 + 3,895 =$ ⬚

6. $6,959 + 9,817 + 8,884 =$ ⬚

Name _____

Date _____ Class _____

Score /30

Addition of Fractions

Before fractions can be added they must be changed into fractions of the same type. This is done by finding the smallest number that the denominators will divide into without leaving a remainder. This number is known as the Lowest Common Denominator (LCD). If the answer to the problem has a value greater than 1, it is improper and must be changed into a mixed fraction which consists of whole numbers and fractions.

A.   Add these fractions. Some of the answers are improper fractions so they will have to be changed into mixed fractions.

1. $\dfrac{5}{6} + \dfrac{2}{3} = \boxed{}$

2. $\dfrac{3}{10} + \dfrac{2}{5} = \boxed{}$

3. $\dfrac{4}{5} + \dfrac{2}{3} = \boxed{}$

4. $\dfrac{1}{3} + \dfrac{1}{5} = \boxed{}$

5. $\dfrac{1}{4} + \dfrac{5}{8} = \boxed{}$

6. $\dfrac{5}{8} + \dfrac{3}{4} = \boxed{}$

7. $\dfrac{3}{8} + \dfrac{3}{4} = \boxed{}$

8. $\dfrac{1}{3} + \dfrac{3}{4} = \boxed{}$

9. $\dfrac{1}{4} + \dfrac{1}{3} = \boxed{}$

10. $\dfrac{2}{3} + \dfrac{5}{12} = \boxed{}$

11. $\dfrac{1}{2} + \dfrac{3}{4} = \boxed{}$

12. $\dfrac{1}{12} + \dfrac{5}{6} = \boxed{}$

13. $\dfrac{1}{8} + \dfrac{3}{4} = \boxed{}$

14. $\dfrac{1}{2} + \dfrac{1}{3} = \boxed{}$

15. $\dfrac{2}{3} + \dfrac{1}{2} = \boxed{}$

When adding mixed fractions, add the whole numbers first. Then follow the same procedure as in Section A with the remaining fractions.

B.   Solve these problems. Make sure there are no improper fractions in the answers.

1. $3\dfrac{3}{4} + 4\dfrac{1}{8} = \boxed{}$

2. $1\dfrac{5}{6} + 4\dfrac{1}{3} = \boxed{}$

3. $4\dfrac{1}{4} + 5\dfrac{3}{8} = \boxed{}$

4. $2\dfrac{1}{4} + 1\dfrac{1}{5} = \boxed{}$

5. $\dfrac{1}{14} + 5\dfrac{3}{7} = \boxed{}$

6. $2\dfrac{3}{8} + 3\dfrac{1}{4} = \boxed{}$

7. $3\dfrac{4}{9} + 2\dfrac{2}{3} = \boxed{}$

8. $\dfrac{2}{3} + 4\dfrac{1}{3} = \boxed{}$

9. $2\dfrac{1}{10} + 6\dfrac{3}{5} = \boxed{}$

10. $9\dfrac{1}{4} + 1\dfrac{1}{2} = \boxed{}$

11. $1\dfrac{1}{2} + 3\dfrac{1}{2} = \boxed{}$

12. $4\dfrac{1}{3} + 2\dfrac{3}{5} = \boxed{}$

13. $5\dfrac{1}{2} + 2\dfrac{3}{4} = \boxed{}$

14. $4\dfrac{3}{5} + 1\dfrac{1}{4} = \boxed{}$

15. $2\dfrac{1}{8} + 5\dfrac{3}{4} = \boxed{}$

Subtraction of Fractions

 Before fractions can be subtracted they must be changed into fractions of the same type. This is done by finding the smallest number that the denominators will divide into without leaving a remainder. This is known as the Lowest Common Denominator (LCD).

For example, to subtract $\frac{1}{2}$ from $\frac{3}{5}$ do this: choose 10 as the LCD for the denominators. Change $\frac{3}{5}$ to $\frac{6}{10}$ and $\frac{1}{2}$ to $\frac{5}{10}$. So, $\frac{6}{10} - \frac{5}{10} = \frac{1}{10}$.
Thus, $\frac{3}{5} - \frac{1}{2} = \frac{1}{10}$. Easy! Now do the problems in Section A the same way.

A.   Complete these subtraction problems. You might find it useful to do your work on a separate piece of paper.

1. $\frac{3}{4} - \frac{1}{8} = \boxed{}$ 6. $\frac{1}{3} - \frac{1}{4} = \boxed{}$ 11. $\frac{5}{6} - \frac{2}{3} = \boxed{}$

2. $\frac{2}{3} - \frac{1}{2} = \boxed{}$ 7. $\frac{4}{5} - \frac{2}{3} = \boxed{}$ 12. $\frac{3}{4} - \frac{1}{2} = \boxed{}$

3. $\frac{1}{2} - \frac{1}{3} = \boxed{}$ 8. $\frac{2}{5} - \frac{3}{10} = \boxed{}$ 13. $\frac{7}{9} - \frac{1}{3} = \boxed{}$

4. $\frac{5}{6} - \frac{1}{5} = \boxed{}$ 9. $\frac{4}{5} - \frac{3}{4} = \boxed{}$ 14. $\frac{1}{2} - \frac{1}{8} = \boxed{}$

5. $\frac{3}{4} - \frac{2}{5} = \boxed{}$ 10. $\frac{3}{7} - \frac{1}{3} = \boxed{}$ 15. $\frac{1}{3} - \frac{1}{5} = \boxed{}$

 When subtracting mixed fractions, subtract the whole numbers first.
Then follow the same procedure as in Section A with the remaining fractions.
Give your answers in their lowest terms.

B.   Solve these calculations.

1. $5\frac{3}{4} - 2\frac{1}{2} = \boxed{}$ 6. $4\frac{3}{4} - 3\frac{1}{8} = \boxed{}$ 11. $2\frac{1}{4} - 1\frac{1}{5} = \boxed{}$

2. $5\frac{3}{8} - 4\frac{1}{4} = \boxed{}$ 7. $6\frac{3}{5} - 2\frac{1}{10} = \boxed{}$ 12. $4\frac{3}{5} - 1\frac{1}{4} = \boxed{}$

3. $7\frac{1}{4} - 3\frac{1}{8} = \boxed{}$ 8. $4\frac{5}{6} - 1\frac{1}{3} = \boxed{}$ 13. $3\frac{2}{3} - 2\frac{4}{9} = \boxed{}$

4. $3\frac{3}{8} - 2\frac{1}{4} = \boxed{}$ 9. $4\frac{2}{3} - 2\frac{1}{3} = \boxed{}$ 14. $4\frac{3}{5} - 2\frac{1}{3} = \boxed{}$

5. $3\frac{1}{2} - 1\frac{1}{2} = \boxed{}$ 10. $3\frac{3}{7} - 2\frac{1}{14} = \boxed{}$ 15. $5\frac{3}{4} - 2\frac{1}{8} = \boxed{}$

Number

Name _____

Date _____   Class _____

Score   /36

Subtraction of Whole Numbers

In each section of this worksheet, two numbers are given for each problem. Subtract the smallest of these from the largest. Before writing the answer you should do the problems on a separate piece of paper.

A.   Complete these problems. They all have borrowing from the tens and hundreds columns.

1.   1,295, 4,911 _____   4.   5,716, 1,179 _____   7.   6,072, 7,531 _____

2.   6,834, 5,675 _____   5.   7,821, 6,296 _____   8.   1,114, 2,913 _____

3.   5,587, 8,736 _____   6.   2,089, 9,513 _____   9.   5,822, 7,921 _____

B.   Now try these. They all have borrowing from the hundreds and thousands columns.

1.   9,250, 3,890 _____   4.   2,591, 6,588 _____   7.   4,694, 8,577 _____

2.   3,449, 1,965 _____   5.   1,461, 6,229 _____   8.   4,695, 7,637 _____

3.   9,232, 6,380 _____   6.   3,751, 8,148 _____   9.   2,452, 6,435 _____

C.   Something harder! All of these problems have borrowing from 3 columns.

1.   7,635, 9,314 _____   4.   9,627, 1,839 _____   7.   7,896, 8,122 _____

2.   5,887, 7,273 _____   5.   5,162, 2,399 _____   8.   4,388, 9,353 _____

3.   7,214, 6,457 _____   6.   6,831, 4,997 _____   9.   4,213, 1,446 _____

D.   Finally, these problems all involve subtraction from zero.

1.   6,466, 7,007 _____   4.   8,700, 4,018 _____   7.   2,852, 4,000 _____

2.   8,900, 3,615 _____   5.   7,400, 2,187 _____   8.   6,734, 7,000 _____

3.   6,006, 2,423 _____   6.   1,673, 8,007 _____   9.   4,586, 9,800 _____

Name _____

Date _____ Class _____

Score

/ 30

Multiplication of Fractions

 To multiply fractions is quite simple. All you have to do is multiply the numerators together and multiply the denominators together. You can sometimes make the work easier by reducing. You may reduce any number on the top with any number underneath either before or after you multiply.

For example: $\frac{6}{8}$ x $\frac{2}{4}$ with reducing becomes $\frac{3}{4}$ x $\frac{1}{2}$ = $\frac{3}{8}$.

If you are multiplying a fraction by a whole number simply multiply the numerator by the number, reduce and make the improper fraction into a mixed fraction.

A. Complete these multiplication problems. You might find it useful to do them on a separate piece of paper.

1. $\frac{1}{2}$ x $\frac{2}{5}$ = ☐

2. $\frac{7}{8}$ x 2 = ☐

3. $\frac{2}{3}$ x $\frac{4}{8}$ = ☐

4. $\frac{3}{4}$ x $\frac{1}{3}$ = ☐

5. 3 x $\frac{4}{6}$ = ☐

6. $\frac{6}{8}$ x $\frac{3}{6}$ = ☐

7. $\frac{1}{6}$ x $\frac{3}{4}$ = ☐

8. $\frac{2}{6}$ x 5 = ☐

9. $\frac{3}{4}$ x $\frac{2}{3}$ = ☐

10. $\frac{3}{8}$ x $\frac{3}{10}$ = ☐

11. $\frac{1}{4}$ x $\frac{2}{3}$ = ☐

12. $\frac{5}{6}$ x 4 = ☐

13. $\frac{4}{10}$ x $\frac{4}{5}$ = ☐

14. $\frac{3}{5}$ x $\frac{2}{10}$ = ☐

15. $\frac{5}{10}$ x $\frac{1}{4}$ = ☐

 If you are multiplying mixed fractions, first make them improper. Then follow the same procedure as in Section A. Remember to change your answer back into a mixed fraction.

B. Solve these problems.

1. $\frac{2}{3}$ x $1\frac{1}{5}$ = ☐

2. $1\frac{1}{2}$ x $\frac{1}{2}$ = ☐

3. $1\frac{1}{2}$ x $\frac{2}{3}$ = ☐

4. $1\frac{4}{6}$ x $2\frac{2}{8}$ = ☐

5. $5\frac{2}{5}$ x $\frac{5}{9}$ = ☐

6. $\frac{1}{9}$ x $4\frac{1}{2}$ = ☐

7. $1\frac{1}{3}$ x $1\frac{1}{2}$ = ☐

8. $2\frac{1}{2}$ x $\frac{2}{5}$ = ☐

9. $\frac{4}{5}$ x $2\frac{1}{2}$ = ☐

10. $1\frac{1}{4}$ x $\frac{1}{5}$ = ☐

11. $\frac{3}{5}$ x $1\frac{1}{4}$ = ☐

12. $3\frac{1}{2}$ x $4\frac{1}{7}$ = ☐

13. $\frac{21}{25}$ x $7\frac{1}{7}$ = ☐

14. $3\frac{1}{2}$ x $\frac{4}{7}$ = ☐

15. $\frac{8}{21}$ x $3\frac{1}{2}$ = ☐

Number

Name _____

Date _____ Class _____

Division of Fractions

Dividing fractions is quite simple. All you have to do is turn the divisor upside down and then multiply the numerators together and multiply the denominators together. You may only reduce any number on top with any number underneath when you have turned the divisor upside down.

For example: $\frac{6}{8} \div \frac{2}{4}$ becomes $\frac{6}{8} \times \frac{4}{2}$ which, with reducing, becomes $\frac{3}{4} \times \frac{2}{1} = \frac{6}{4} = 1\frac{1}{2}$. If you are dividing a fraction by a whole number, simply write the whole number over 1 and then follow the same procedure.

A. Complete these division problems. You might find it useful to do them out on a separate piece of paper.

1. $\frac{4}{5} \div \frac{2}{7} = \boxed{}$ 6. $\frac{2}{5} \div \frac{3}{5} = \boxed{}$ 11. $\frac{1}{2} \div \frac{1}{4} = \boxed{}$

2. $\frac{4}{9} \div \frac{1}{3} = \boxed{}$ 7. $\frac{5}{9} \div \frac{2}{3} = \boxed{}$ 12. $\frac{1}{2} \div \frac{5}{12} = \boxed{}$

3. $\frac{3}{4} \div \frac{1}{2} = \boxed{}$ 8. $\frac{2}{3} \div \frac{1}{3} = \boxed{}$ 13. $\frac{3}{5} \div \frac{9}{20} = \boxed{}$

4. $\frac{1}{2} \div \frac{1}{3} = \boxed{}$ 9. $\frac{1}{3} \div \frac{1}{4} = \boxed{}$ 14. $\frac{3}{4} \div \frac{5}{16} = \boxed{}$

5. $\frac{6}{11} \div \frac{3}{22} = \boxed{}$ 10. $\frac{5}{6} \div \frac{2}{3} = \boxed{}$ 15. $\frac{7}{8} \div \frac{5}{16} = \boxed{}$

If you are dividing mixed fractions first make them improper. Then follow the same procedure as in Section A. Remember to change your answer into a mixed fraction.

B. Solve these problems.

1. $6\frac{1}{2} \div 4\frac{1}{3} = \boxed{}$ 6. $3\frac{1}{3} \div 1\frac{2}{3} = \boxed{}$ 11. $3\frac{1}{4} \div 4\frac{1}{3} = \boxed{}$

2. $\frac{5}{12} \div 2\frac{1}{2} = \boxed{}$ 7. $2\frac{1}{3} \div \frac{7}{8} = \boxed{}$ 12. $2\frac{1}{2} \div \frac{1}{2} = \boxed{}$

3. $2\frac{1}{2} \div 1\frac{1}{4} = \boxed{}$ 8. $1\frac{3}{4} \div \frac{1}{8} = \boxed{}$ 13. $1\frac{1}{4} \div 1\frac{1}{2} = \boxed{}$

4. $1\frac{1}{2} \div \frac{3}{7} = \boxed{}$ 9. $\frac{7}{8} \div 1\frac{5}{16} = \boxed{}$ 14. $3\frac{3}{4} \div \frac{5}{16} = \boxed{}$

5. $5\frac{1}{3} \div \frac{4}{9} = \boxed{}$ 10. $3\frac{1}{3} \div \frac{5}{9} = \boxed{}$ 15. $1\frac{7}{8} \div 1\frac{1}{4} = \boxed{}$

Decimal Addition

→ Addition of decimal numbers is easy. Your numbers should be written in columns with the decimal points in line. If you are adding some whole numbers, put a decimal point at the end of the whole number and add zeros as required. The decimal point in the answer goes underneath the other decimal points.

A. Do problems in this chart in columns on a separate piece of paper.
Transfer your answers to the chart. Remember to keep the decimal points in line.

1.	94.87	+	81.47	=	11.	32.37	+	97.59	=
2.	46.31	+	16	=	12.	40.98	+	99.05	=
3.	82.65	+	28.34	=	13.	27	+	54.89	=
4.	97.01	+	15.91	=	14.	57.15	+	43	=
5.	37	+	24.17	=	15.	21.30	+	27.48	=
6.	85.66	+	60.24	=	16.	42.78	+	46.33	=
7.	59.98	+	54.09	=	17.	69	+	30.88	=
8.	58	+	33.70	=	18.	88.71	+	76.94	=
9.	57.45	+	72.52	=	19.	69.89	+	75	=
10.	24.82	+	93	=	20.	53.21	+	83.79	=

B. The calculations in this next chart are a little harder.
Once again, remember to keep the decimal points in line.

1.	60.06	+	7.8	+	2	+	24.1	=
2.	49	+	8.0	+	69.80	+	127.50	=
3.	35.6	+	182.30	+	47	+	9.8	=
4.	8.00	+	94.56	+	8.9	+	97	=
5.	61	+	7.02	+	92.71	+	393	=
6.	884.3	+	72	+	6.0	+	40.50	=
7.	79.85	+	67	+	912	+	9.30	=
8.	6.90	+	0.09	+	18.0	+	593.8	=

Name _____

Date _____ Class _____

Decimal Subtraction

➡ Subtraction of decimal numbers is easy. Your numbers should be written in columns with the decimal points in line. If you are subtracting some whole numbers, put a decimal point at the end of the whole number and add zeros as required. The Section A answers can be checked by adding the answer to the smaller number. The result should be the larger number in the original problem. Complete the problems in the same way as whole number subtraction.

A. Do the problems on this chart in columns on a separate piece of paper. Transfer your answers to the chart. Don't forget to check your answers.

1.	60.02	–	43.22	=		10.	90	–	29.72	=
2.	97.00	–	51.21	=		11.	890	–	265.7	=
3.	82.69	–	34.92	=		12.	58	–	29.67	=
4.	56	–	20.97	=		13.	5.00	–	3.37	=
5.	96.42	–	28	=		14.	7.60	–	5.03	=
6.	34.86	–	18.95	=		15.	50.09	–	2.45	=
7.	40	–	23.16	=		16.	74.20	–	28.5	=
8.	382.3	–	36.79	=		17.	65	–	32.68	=
9.	85.15	–	7.65	=		18.	90.08	–	18.41	=

B. These next calculations are a little more difficult.

1.	83.90	–	2.39	–	10.6	–	8.04	=	
2.	300.4	–	5	–	29.93	–	6.00	=	
3.	4.34	–	0.62	–	0.93	–	1.92	=	
4.	104.56	–	9.5	–	8.79	–	69	=	
5.	50.03	–	4.90	–	9.50	–	8	=	
6.	352.80	–	65.62	–	28.71	–	0.25	=	
7.	104.60	–	67.9	–	8.85	–	9.24	=	
8.	11.02	–	5.10	–	0.99	–	2	=	
9.	100.56	–	28.7	–	0.95	–	9.67	=	

Name _____

Date _____ Class _____

Score

/36

Multiplication of Whole Numbers

Before writing the answer for each problem on this worksheet, you should do the problems on a separate piece of paper.
You will need to know your 2x to 10x tables to complete all the calculations on this worksheet.

A. All the problems in this section require knowledge of your 4x and 5x tables.

1. 5,445 x 9 =

2. 3,524 x 5 =

3. 4,795 x 4 =

4. 5 x 4,060 =

5. 4 x 4,213 =

6. 7 x 4,545 =

7. 8,771 x 5 =

8. 4 x 6,280 =

9. 2,359 x 5 =

B. For this section, your 6x and 7x tables are needed.

1. 8,268 x 7 =

2. 3,195 x 7 =

3. 6,700 x 8 =

4. 2 x 6,767 =

5. 9,263 x 6 =

6. 3 x 7,667 =

7. 9 x 6,007 =

8. 6 x 5,805 =

9. 5,342 x 7 =

C. Your 8x and 9x tables will be useful when you complete these calculations.

1. 1,246 x 8 =

2. 9,098 x 2 =

3. 6,479 x 8 =

4. 9 x 8,889 =

5. 5,386 x 8 =

6. 9 x 1,475 =

7. 5 x 8,900 =

8. 9 x 8,102 =

9. 8,958 x 8 =

D. If you are a 2x to 10x tables expert, you'll have no trouble with these.

1. 7,051 x 2 =

2. 1,296 x 4 =

3. 9 x 3,684 =

4. 2 x 8,623 =

5. 6 x 3,682 =

6. 3,210 x 8 =

7. 5 x 8,001 =

8. 1,783 x 7 =

9. 10 x 2,758 =

Decimal Multiplication

Write the problem in the same way as a long-multiplication calculation and multiply the numbers as if they had no decimal points. Then add the number of decimal places in the first number to the number of decimal places in the second number, count over that many places from the right in your answer and place your decimal point there.

For example, 1.23 x 2.4 would be multiplied as 123 x 24 = 2,952. The total number of decimal places in the top and bottom numbers is 3 so the answer is 2.952.

Do the problems in this chart in columns on a separate piece of paper. Transfer your answers to the chart. Remember to place the decimal point in your answers.

1.	82.4	x	27	=		19.	6.3	x	976	=
2.	0.75	x	2.31	=		20.	8.28	x	23	=
3.	67	x	0.556	=		21.	856	x	4.2	=
4.	97.4	x	2.8	=		22.	6.4	x	0.224	=
5.	754	x	0.11	=		23.	0.313	x	0.32	=
6.	7.9	x	2.53	=		24.	7.3	x	3.41	=
7.	31.1	x	0.51	=		25.	0.68	x	715	=
8.	0.78	x	65.4	=		26.	136	x	1.4	=
9.	59	x	19.4	=		27.	8.4	x	46.5	=
10.	0.639	x	3.6	=		28.	6.57	x	4.3	=
11.	82	x	46.2	=		29.	479	x	0.34	=
12.	0.88	x	0.255	=		30.	2.46	x	1.5	=
13.	5.56	x	0.19	=		31.	0.58	x	0.379	=
14.	8.6	x	0.317	=		32.	5.97	x	45	=
15.	87.7	x	5.6	=		33.	82.496	x	0.797	=
16.	0.95	x	952	=		34.	15.7	x	0.25	=
17.	0.707	x	37	=		35.	9.1	x	145	=
18.	0.94	x	5.07	=		36.	6.95	x	0.48	=

Name _____

Date _____ Class _____

Score

/26

Decimal Division

When you divide a decimal number by 10 or 100 or 1,000 you move the decimal point one or two or three place(s) to the left.

For example, 4.7 ÷ 10 = 0.47, 4.7 ÷ 100 = 0.047 and 4.7 ÷ 1,000 = 0.0047
Notice how adding zeros changes the decimal place of the 4 and 7.

A. **Write the answers to these questions in the empty boxes in the chart.**

1.	24.5	÷	100	=		5.	0.02	÷	100	=
2.	48.7	÷	10	=		6.	7.83	÷	10	=
3.	0.371	÷	10	=		7.	3.4	÷	1,000	=
4.	0.35	÷	100	=		8.	220.08	÷	1,000	=

To divide a decimal number by a whole number, do the problem in the same way as a division problem with only whole numbers. Remember to keep the decimal point in your answer in line with the decimal point in the problem.

B. **Now try these! Remember to keep your decimal points in line vertically.**

1.	95.4	÷	3	=		5.	4.76	÷	2	=
2.	0.876	÷	6	=		6.	0.590	÷	5	=
3.	1.47	÷	7	=		7.	81.6	÷	8	=
4.	5.90	÷	5	=		8.	0.954	÷	9	=

To divide a decimal number by a decimal number, move the decimal point the same number of places to the right in both numbers until the second number is a whole number and then proceed as in Section B.

For example, 0.495 ÷ 0.5 = 4.95 ÷ 5 = 0.99

C. **Now try these!**

1.	8.74	÷	1.9	=		6.	68.8	÷	0.16	=
2.	0.408	÷	0.24	=		7.	6.09	÷	0.29	=
3.	53.3	÷	4.1	=		8.	0.442	÷	1.7	=
4.	6.75	÷	0.27	=		9.	1.024	÷	3.2	=
5.	0.999	÷	0.27	=		10.	6.72	÷	2.4	=

Name _____

Date _____ Class _____

Division of Whole Numbers

Before writing the answer for each problem on this worksheet you should write and complete the problems on a separate piece of paper. You will need to know your 2x to 10x tables to complete the calculations.

A. **All of the problems in this section require knowledge of your 4x and 5x tables.**

1. $5,728 \div 4 =$ ☐
2. $8,000 \div 4 =$ ☐
3. $4,000 \div 5 =$ ☐

4. $5,125 \div 5 =$ ☐
5. $7,405 \div 5 =$ ☐
6. $3,692 \div 4 =$ ☐

7. $7,185 \div 5 =$ ☐
8. $9,864 \div 4 =$ ☐
9. $7,560 \div 5 =$ ☐

B. **For this section, your 6x and 7x tables are needed.**

1. $8,100 \div 6 =$ ☐
2. $9,730 \div 7 =$ ☐
3. $9,000 \div 6 =$ ☐

4. $4,782 \div 6 =$ ☐
5. $8,099 \div 7 =$ ☐
6. $9,144 \div 6 =$ ☐

7. $2,856 \div 7 =$ ☐
8. $8,454 \div 6 =$ ☐
9. $4,557 \div 7 =$ ☐

C. **Your 8x and 9x tables will be useful when you solve these problems.**

1. $8,520 \div 8 =$ ☐
2. $9,486 \div 9 =$ ☐
3. $5,000 \div 8 =$ ☐

4. $9,000 \div 9 =$ ☐
5. $3,264 \div 8 =$ ☐
6. $1,854 \div 9 =$ ☐

7. $2,696 \div 8 =$ ☐
8. $7,056 \div 9 =$ ☐
9. $9,576 \div 8 =$ ☐

D. **If you are a 2x to 10x tables expert, you will have no trouble with these problems.**

1. $8,250 \div 5 =$ ☐
2. $7,854 \div 7 =$ ☐
3. $6,468 \div 6 =$ ☐

4. $6,120 \div 4 =$ ☐
5. $5,106 \div 2 =$ ☐
6. $5,312 \div 8 =$ ☐

7. $5,238 \div 9 =$ ☐
8. $8,120 \div 10 =$ ☐
9. $6,252 \div 3 =$ ☐

Name _____

Date _____ Class _____

Score

/12

Averages

➡️ The average, or arithmetic mean, of a set of numbers is the total of the numbers divided by the amount of numbers in the set.
Remember this when doing the problems on this worksheet.

Answer these questions.

1. The individual weights of six oranges are 120 g, 108 g, 114 g, 96 g, 104 g and 130 g.
   What is their mean weight?

2. Find the average of 14.2, 18.5, 15.3, 16.7 and 13.8.

3. Nine numbers have an average of 29.
   What is their total?

4. Colin scored 43, 36, 47, 29, 45, 49 and 38 on his math tests.
   What was his average score?

5. Helen scored 32, 48, 27, 46, 40,
   42 and 49 out of 50 on her science tests.
   What was her average score?

6. Four children have an average age of 9 years 3 months.
   What is their total age in years?

7. Four children are aged 11 years 6 months, 11 years 3 months, 11 years 9 months and 11 years 2 months.
   Find their average age and write your answer in months.

8. Two boxes weigh 60 g and 70 g. What must the weight of a third box be if the average weight of the three boxes is 60 g?

9. What is the average of nine eights, six elevens and seven sixes?

10. Find the arithmetic mean of 18 km, 5 km, 26 km, 38 km, 14 km, 56 km, 33 km and 2 km.

11. Twelve numbers have an average of 59.
    What is their total?

12. A family of four buys on average 2 liters of milk per day.
    How many liters of milk will they buy in a normal year?

Four Rules Problems

➡ To find the answers to most of these problems you will have to do addition, subtraction, multiplication or division on a separate piece of paper.
For some questions you will have to use more than one calculation to find the answer.

Solve these problems.

1. A container full of water weighs 16 kg. When half full it weighs 10 kg. What is the weight of the container when empty?

2. How many times is 9 cm contained in 4 m 86 cm?

3. Find the value of 180 x 26 ÷ 13.

4. A piece of string is $8\frac{3}{5}$ meters long.
   Another piece is $\frac{3}{4}$ of the length of the first piece.
   What is the total length in meters and centimeters of the two pieces of string? _____

5. From $200 subtract 15 times $4.56. _____

6. Express 2,463 mm in meters, centimeters and millimeters. _____

7. Find the cost of 27 kg of sugar priced at $0.76 for 2 kilograms. _____

8. Three-fifths of a sum of money is $44.01. What is the sum of money?

9. (a) A family found they could travel 30 km in their car on 5 liters of gas costing $0.60 per liter. What would be the cost of a journey of 150 km at this rate? _____

   (b) If they found a gas station where gas was 10% cheaper, how much would be saved on the cost of the journey? _____

10. Add all the odd numbers between 10 and 26.

11. Find the difference between the sum of the odd numbers between 10 and 26 and the sum of the even numbers between 13 and 29.

12. How much less than 2 is the sum of $\frac{1}{2} + 1 + \frac{1}{8} + \frac{1}{4}$?

Name _____

Date _____   Class _____

Score

/19

Crossnumbers

Crossnumber puzzles are like crossword puzzles, only the clues are problems and the answers are numbers. You may need to do the problems on a separate piece of paper. You may check your answers with a calculator.

ACROSS

1. 12 x 1,894
3. 216 ÷ 8
4. 364 ÷ 7
5. 2 x 2,006 x 2
7. 8,824 ÷ 2
9. 8,640 ÷ 4
11. 2 x 3 x 6
14. 48 + 78
15. 8,762 − 1,559 − 3,679
16. 132 ÷ 12

DOWN

1. 6,849 + 6,217 + 5,238 + 5,528
2. 7,128 ÷ 9
3. 6,740 + 5,964 + 9,728
6. 10 x 2 x 205
8. 9,651 + 8,774 − 2,993 + 7,236
10. 228 ÷ 12
12. 215 + 141 + 205
13. 3 x 31
14. 63 − 49

Probability

Name _____

Date _____ Class _____

Score ___ / 6

From Certainty to Impossibility

➡ Probability is the likelihood of an event happening.
All events can be classified into the following six groups:
(1) certain (2) very likely (3) likely (4) unlikely (5) very unlikely and (6) impossible.

In the boxes below, write a sentence or two to describe an event in which you are not involved but which would fit into each of the topic headings.

1. Certain to happen

2. Very likely to happen

3. Likely to happen

4. Unlikely to happen

5. Very unlikely to happen

6. Impossible

What Are Your Chances of...?

 Probability is the likelihood of something happening. It asks the question: What chance is there that a particular event will occur? When we talk of chance we make comments such as: there is a 1 in 5 chance of something happening. This means the event is unlikely to occur. As a fraction we would write 1 in 5 as $\frac{1}{5}$.

A normal pack of playing cards has 4 suits—hearts, clubs, spades and diamonds—each with 13 cards. Each suit has an ace, plain cards numbered 2 to 9, and 3 picture cards—Jack, Queen and King. Hearts and diamonds are red, clubs and spades are black. A pack of shuffled cards has been placed face down on the table. Answer the questions by choosing the most suitable alternative from the possible answers listed and circling it.

What is the chance of turning over:

1. a red card? $\frac{1}{2}$ $\frac{1}{4}$ $\frac{1}{8}$ $\frac{1}{12}$

2. a five? $\frac{1}{5}$ $\frac{1}{13}$ $\frac{1}{8}$ $\frac{1}{7}$

3. a club? $\frac{1}{4}$ $\frac{1}{10}$ $\frac{1}{2}$ $\frac{1}{3}$

4. a red king? $\frac{1}{9}$ $\frac{1}{7}$ $\frac{1}{26}$ $\frac{1}{8}$

5. a black ace? $\frac{1}{3}$ $\frac{1}{4}$ $\frac{1}{26}$ $\frac{1}{8}$

6. ace of clubs? $\frac{1}{9}$ $\frac{1}{52}$ $\frac{1}{3}$ $\frac{1}{8}$

7. a king? $\frac{1}{8}$ $\frac{1}{4}$ $\frac{1}{13}$ $\frac{1}{3}$

8. a diamond? $\frac{1}{4}$ $\frac{1}{2}$ $\frac{1}{15}$ $\frac{1}{6}$

9. a black queen? $\frac{1}{9}$ $\frac{1}{26}$ $\frac{1}{5}$ $\frac{1}{3}$

10. a red ace? $\frac{1}{9}$ $\frac{1}{26}$ $\frac{1}{5}$ $\frac{1}{3}$

11. a black card? $\frac{1}{52}$ $\frac{1}{2}$ $\frac{1}{7}$ $\frac{1}{3}$

12. two of spades? $\frac{1}{52}$ $\frac{1}{6}$ $\frac{1}{4}$ $\frac{1}{9}$

13. an ace? $\frac{1}{9}$ $\frac{1}{13}$ $\frac{1}{2}$ $\frac{1}{6}$

14. a ten? $\frac{1}{13}$ $\frac{1}{4}$ $\frac{1}{7}$ $\frac{1}{9}$

15. a heart? $\frac{1}{26}$ $\frac{1}{4}$ $\frac{1}{5}$ $\frac{1}{8}$

16. a queen? $\frac{1}{2}$ $\frac{1}{8}$ $\frac{1}{13}$ $\frac{1}{5}$

17. a spade? $\frac{1}{13}$ $\frac{1}{3}$ $\frac{1}{4}$ $\frac{1}{9}$

18. a red jack? $\frac{1}{4}$ $\frac{1}{7}$ $\frac{1}{8}$ $\frac{1}{26}$

Only a Matter of Time!

➡ There are sixty seconds in one minute, sixty minutes in one hour and twenty-four hours in one day.

Answer these questions.

1. An airplane departs at 18:56 and arrives at its destination 4 hours 24 minutes later. What is the time of its arrival? _____

2. Jane was born on June 1, 1986. Paul was born on September 1, 1988. Write the ages in years and months of both children on January 1, 1997. _____ _____

3. A raffle ticket was bought on April 2. The drawing for the prizes took place on May 11. How many days after the ticket was bought was this? _____

4. Edward was born on April 21, 1989. He is 3 years and 4 months older than Kate. What is Kate's date of birth? _____

5. A superstore opens from 8 a.m. until 7 p.m. Monday to Saturday and from 10 a.m. until 4.30 p.m. on Sunday. How many hours is it open over a two-week period? _____

6. A long-distance coach leaves Albany at 0609 and arrives in New York City at 0922. How many hours and minutes does the journey take? _____

7. What is the time 12 hours and 20 minutes before 0910? _____

8. Each day a woman works from 8:15 a.m. to 11:45 a.m. and from 12:45 p.m. to 4:15 p.m. How many hours does she work in 5 days? _____

9. A man works for 39 hours from Monday to Saturday inclusive. What is the average time in hours and minutes he works each day? _____

10. How long will it take a walker to travel 21 km if he or she averages 3.5 km per hour? _____

Before, After and Between

➡️ There are sixty seconds in one minute, sixty minutes in one hour and twenty-four hours in one day. Write your answer in the same way as expressed in the question.

A. Answer these questions. What is the time:

1. 24 min before 1:10 p.m.? _____
2. 52 min before 6:15 a.m.? _____
3. 49 min before 11:36 p.m.? _____
4. 71 min before 3:12 a.m.? _____

5. 18 min before 8:24 a.m.? _____
6. 36 min before 12:10 p.m.? _____
7. 63 min before 12:55 a.m.? _____
8. 85 min before 7:56 p.m.? _____

B. Now try these. What is the time:

1. 37 minutes after 0520? ☐
2. 26 minutes after 1533? ☐
3. 49 minutes after 1114? ☐
4. 65 minutes after 2142? ☐
5. 52 minutes after 1011? ☐
6. 74 minutes after 2356? ☐
7. 81 minutes after 1402? ☐
8. 98 minutes after 1929? ☐

C. Find the difference in minutes between the two times given.

1. 6:15 p.m. and 7:29 p.m. _____
2. 0513 and 0612 _____
3. 4:18 p.m. and 6:30 p.m. _____
4. 2033 and 2331 _____

5. 2335 and 0049 _____
6. 10:23 a.m. and 12:06 p.m. _____
7. 9:55 p.m. and 12:17 a.m. _____
8. 1738 and 1926 _____

Volume and Capacity

Name _____

Date _____ Class _____

Score / 16

Volume Calculations

Volume is the amount of space taken by a solid object.
It is measured in cubic units. Cubic millimeters (mm^3), cubic centimeters (cm^3) and cubic meters (m^3) are all common cubic units. To find the volume of a rectangular-shaped object like a box you use length x width x height.

Before finding the volume in this way you must first make sure all sides are measured using the same units.

A. Find the volumes of the rectangular prisms whose sizes are given on the chart below. The sizes given on the chart are not all in the same units so you will have some thinking to do!

Prism	Length	Width	Height	Volume in cubic cm (cm^3)
A	5.5 cm	50 mm	3 cm	
B	6 cm	0.05 m	30 mm	
C	30 mm	3.5 cm	5 cm	
D	0.04 m	4 cm	60 mm	
E	3 cm	5.5 cm	20 mm	
F	50 mm	0.06 m	4 cm	
G	30 mm	6 cm	0.04 m	
H	5.5 cm	3 cm	70 mm	
I	4 cm	0.02 m	60 mm	
J	3 cm	4.5 cm	50 mm	

B. Using your results from Section A, write the volume in cm^3 of the following.

1. four times prism C _____

2. nine times prism H _____

3. six times prism A _____

4. seven times prism J _____

5. five times prism G _____

6. eight times prism D _____

Capacity Calculations

Capacity is the amount of space that a liquid takes up.
It is measured in milliliters (ml) and liters (L). For the problems below,
write your first answer in liters and milliliters and your second answer in liters to
three decimal places.

A. Solve these addition and subtraction problems.

1. 4,275 ml + 3,652 ml + 321 ml   [ ] L [ ] ml or [ ] L

2. 93 ml + 912 ml + 7,885 ml + 67 ml   [ ] L [ ] ml or [ ] L

3. 9,659 ml – 72 ml – 6 ml – 405 ml   [ ] L [ ] ml or [ ] L

4. 702 ml + 393 ml + 61 ml + 5,271 ml   [ ] L [ ] ml or [ ] L

5. 1,275 ml – 8 ml – 49 ml – 698 ml   [ ] L [ ] ml or [ ] L

6. 233 ml + 48 ml + 6 ml + 8,795 ml   [ ] L [ ] ml or [ ] L

7. 4,076 ml – 633 ml – 88 ml – 2 ml   [ ] L [ ] ml or [ ] L

B. Solve these multiplication and division problems.

1. 1 L 273 ml x 2 x 3   [ ] L [ ] ml or [ ] L

2. 20 L 934 ml ÷ 3 ÷ 3   [ ] L [ ] ml or [ ] L

3. 2 L 839 ml x 3 x 4   [ ] L [ ] ml or [ ] L

4. 23 L 430 ml ÷ 5 ÷ 2   [ ] L [ ] ml or [ ] L

5. 3 L 21 ml x 2 x 4   [ ] L [ ] ml or [ ] L

Volume and Capacity

Name _____

Date _____

Class _____

Score ____/12

Volume and Capacity Problems

Volume usually refers to the amount of space taken up by a solid object. It is measured in cubic millimeters (mm^3), cubic centimeters (cm^3) and cubic meters (m^3). Capacity usually refers to the amount of space taken up by a liquid. It is measured in milliliters (ml) and liters (L).

Solve these problems.

1. A container holds 15 liters of water when full. Find the quantity of water in liters and milliliters when the container is $\frac{3}{4}$ full.

2. A full barrel of oil contained 75 liters. 60% of the oil was then used. How many liters of oil remained?

3. The capacity of a small tank is 3,254 cm^3. How many liters of water does it hold if 1 cm^3 = 1 ml?

4. A jar has a capacity of 325 ml. Find in liters and milliliters the contents of 17 jars.

5. A drum when $\frac{6}{8}$ full holds 72 liters. How many liters does it hold when:
    (a) $\frac{5}{8}$ full? (b) $\frac{1}{8}$ full? (c) $\frac{7}{8}$ full? (d) $\frac{3}{8}$ full?

    (a) [   ]   (b) [   ]   (c) [   ]   (d) [   ]

6. A container has a capacity of 2,200 ml. How many liters is this?

7. Water from a full five-liter container was poured into a jug. When the jug was full, 1 liter 286 ml of water was left in the container. What was the capacity of the jug in cm^3 if 1 cm^3 = 1 ml?

8. If three 5 ml spoonfuls of medicine are taken daily, how many days will a bottle holding 0.195 liters last?

9. What is the volume in m^3 of a cube with a 2.5 meter side?

Name _____

Date _____ Class _____

Right or Wrong

The twins have already done this sheet for you! Unfortunately, they did not remember the information written below and, therefore, some of their answers are wrong. You will have to do the sheet again for them.

1,000 g = 1 kg   1,000 kg = 1 t

Some of the answers in this grid are incorrect. Solve the problems yourself. If the answer is incorrect, write the correct answer in the box next to it. If the answer is correct, put a check mark in the box. Write the correct answer in decimal form in the last box.

1.	7 kg 958 g + 9 kg 665 g =	17 kg 623 g		kg
2.	18 kg 437 g – 3 kg 56 g =	15 kg 381 g		kg
3.	13 kg 243 g x 2 x 3 =	69 kg 385 g		kg
4.	70 kg 860 g ÷ 4 ÷ 5 =	3 kg 543 g		kg
5.	5 t 156 kg + 9 t 728 kg =	14 t 884 kg		t
6.	7.963 kg + 7,847 g =	41 kg 810 g		kg
7.	6 t + 25 kg x 7 =	41 t 155 kg		t
8.	12 t 469 kg – 8 t 571 kg =	3 t 898 kg		t
9.	13,976 kg + 15,354 kg =	29 t 330 kg		t
10.	53 t 24 kg ÷ 2 ÷ 4 =	6 t 628 kg		t
11.	13,459 g – 7 kg 368 g =	6 kg 92 g		kg
12.	48 t 591 kg ÷ 3 ÷ 3 =	5 t 399 kg		t
13.	15 t 638 kg – 11,029 kg =	4 t 690 kg		t
14.	11 t 709 kg x 8 =	93 t 672 kg		t

Weighty Problems!

Weight is a measurement of how heavy something is. It is sometimes referred to as mass. Grams (g), kilograms (kg) and metric tons (t) are common units of weight or mass.

$$1,000 \text{ g} = 1 \text{ kg} \quad 1,000 \text{ kg} = 1 \text{ t}$$

Here are some problems about weight. You may find it easier to work some of them on a separate piece of paper.

1. A metal shelf bracket weighs 200 g. How many brackets would weigh 10 kg?

2. The weight of five 10¢ coins is 32.5 g. What would be the weight in kilograms and grams of 160 of these coins?

3. A bag of sugar weighs 1 kg. If bags are packed eight to a box, how many of these boxes will equal $\frac{1}{5}$ ton?

4. One liter of water weighs 1 kilogram. If a bottle contains 450 ml of water, what would be the weight of water in 20 bottles?

5. The mass of four 5¢ coins is 13 g. The value of 5¢ coins in a bag is $5.60. What is the mass of the coins?

6. The contents of a box have a mass of 1 kg 284 g. Write, in grams, the following fractional amounts of this.
(a) $\frac{1}{2}$ (b) $\frac{3}{4}$ (c) $\frac{2}{3}$ (d) $\frac{4}{6}$ (e) $\frac{5}{12}$ (f) $\frac{2}{6}$

(a)	(b)	(c)	(d)	(e)	(f)

7. The total weight of four parcels is 9 kg 992 g. Parcel A weighs 2,425 g, Parcel B 1,469 g and Parcel C 3,523 g.

   (a) What is the weight in kg and g of Parcel D? _____

   (b) Which two parcels added together equal 5 kg? _____ and _____

Answers

Note: Answers begin on page 6. Where measurement of lines is required, photocopying can create variations that will affect answers.

PAGE 6

A.
1. 120°
2. 73°
3. 51°

B.
1. 55°
2. 63°
3. 38°

C.
1. 161°
2. 56°
3. 113°
4. 71°
5. 128°
6. 92°
7. 28°
8. 159°
9. 144°
10. 105°
11. 13°
12. 36°

D.
1. 83°
2. 22°
3. 45°
4. 18°
5. 31°
6. 56°
7. 54°
8. 49°

PAGE 7

A.
1. 006°
2. 320°
3. 074°
4. 028°
5. 126°
6. 002°
7. 053°
8. 247°

B.
1. 2°
2. 35°

3. 142°
4. 17°
5. 99°
6. 71°
7. 23°
8. 86°

C.
1. 049°
2. 233°
3. 154°
4. 069°
5. 328°
6. 294°

PAGE 8

A.
1. 1,118 cm²
2. 1,675 cm²
3. 1,564 cm²
4. 1,245 cm²
5. 4,462 cm²
6. 4,428 cm²
7. 7,614 cm²
8. 2,025 cm²
9. 8,100 cm²

B.
1. 216 m²
2. 336 m²
3. 512 m²
4. 1,275 m²
5. 627 m²
6. 711 m²

C.
Shape A = 600 mm²
Shape B = 250 mm²
Shape C = 375 mm²
Shape D = 200 mm²
Shape E = 600 mm²
Final = 20.25 cm²

D.
1. 784 km²
2. 2,697 km²
3. 814 km²
4. 4,650 km²
5. 2,688 km²
6. 6,497 km²

PAGE 9

1. 8 m²
2. 4 133 km²
3. 320 cm²
4. 50 m
5. 142 cm²
6. 4
7. 75 m²
8. 30 cm
9. 220 cm²
10. 12 m²

PAGE 10

A. An equilateral parallelogram.
B. rhombus
C. rhombus

PAGE 11

1. school
2. library
3. southwest
4. southeast
5. 1 ¹/₂, 2 ¹/₂, 13 ¹/₂, 7 ¹/₂
6. library
7. 6, 1
8. 3, 7
9. north, west
10. post office and book store

PAGE 12

A.
1. 3,488 miles
2. 8,416 miles
3. 5,824 miles
4. 1,248 miles
5. 1,600 miles
6. 2,720 miles

B.
1. 2,808 miles
2. 1,262 miles

PAGE 13

A.
1. 1/5
2. 40%
3. Red gum
4. 3/5
5. 20%
6. 80%
7. 90°

B.

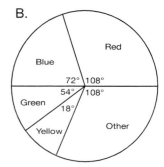

PAGE 14

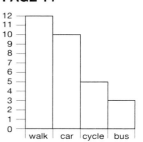

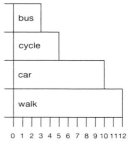

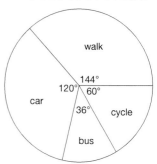

Answers

PAGE 15

A.
1. 42 cm
2. 292 cm
3. 231 cm
4. 195 cm
5. 214 cm
6. 257 cm

B.
1. 2 m 94 cm
2. 32 m 12 cm
3. 18 m 48 cm
4. 23 m 40 cm
5. 19 m 26 cm
6. 38 m 55 cm

C.
1. 32 m 94 cm
2. 5 m 40 cm
3. 16 m 41 cm
4. 20 m 65 cm
5. 23 m 88 cm
6. 14 m 74 cm

D.
1. 3.66 m
2. 0.9 m
3. 5.47 m
4. 2.95 m
5. 5.97 m
6. 7.37 m

PAGE 16

Each drawing should be fully labeled and of the following dimensions.

1. AB – 6 cm
   BC – 2 cm
   CD – 2 cm
   DE – 3 cm
   EF – 1 cm
   FG – 2 cm
   GH – 6 cm
   HI – 2 cm
   IJ – 1 cm
   JK – 3 cm

   KL – 1 cm
   LA - 2 cm

2. AB – 2 cm
   BC – 2 cm
   CD – 5 cm
   DE – 8 cm
   EF – 2.5 cm
   FG – 2 cm
   GH – 4.5 cm
   HI – 2.5 cm
   IJ – 3 cm
   JK – 2.5 cm
   KL – 3 cm
   LA – 3 cm

PAGE 17

A.

Addition of Money					
+	$	$	$	$	$
A	13.75	23.48	26.87	37.87	46.49
18.77	32.52	42.25	45.64	56.64	65.26
27.55	41.30	51.03	54.42	65.42	74.04
35.86	49.61	59.34	62.73	73.73	82.35
44.65	58.40	68.13	71.52	82.52	91.14

B.
1. $45.99
2. $56.77
3. $89.25

C.

Subtraction of Money					
–	$	$	$	$	$
A	19.79	28.32	47.60	63.12	84.45
10.99	8.80	17.33	36.61	52.13	73.46
12.76	7.03	15.56	34.84	50.36	71.69
14.38	5.41	13.94	33.22	48.74	70.07
17.85	1.94	10.47	29.75	45.27	66.60

D.
1. $7.02
2. $3.48
3. $14.56
4. $4.32

PAGE 18

1. $3.89
2. 45¢
3. $11.60
4. 42¢
5. $3.62

6. peaches
7. granulated sugar, chips and cucumbers
8. $31.66

PAGE 19

A.

Multiplication of Money					
×	$	$	$	$	$
A	2.19	3.82	5.37	8.64	10.95
6	13.14	22.92	32.22	51.84	65.70
7	15.33	26.74	37.59	60.48	76.65
8	17.52	30.56	42.96	69.12	87.60
9	19.71	34.38	48.33	77.76	98.55

B.
1. $148.32
2. $267.96
3. $445.44

C.

Division of Money					
÷	$	$	$	$	$
A	121.92	129.60	123.84	1 211.52	125.76
6	20.32	21.60	20.64	201.92	20.96
2	60.96	64.80	61.92	605.76	62.88
4	30.48	32.40	30.96	302.88	31.44
3	40.64	43.20	41.28	403.84	41.92

D.
1. $5.56
2. $6.56
3. $4.05
4. $5.97

PAGE 20

A.
1. 5,987
2. 9,779
3. 8,786
4. 4,871
5. 9,769
6. 5,261

B.
1. 8,821
2. 3,660
3. 7,951
4. 5,730
5. 8,594
6. 7,921

C.
1. 9,376
2. 9,201
3. 9,085
4. 8,359
5. 9,815
6. 9,401

D.
1. 22,432
2. 21,840
3. 23,783
4. 23,175
5. 22,968
6. 25,660

PAGE 21

A.
1. $1 \frac{1}{2}$
2. $\frac{7}{10}$
3. $1 \frac{7}{15}$
4. $\frac{8}{15}$
5. $\frac{7}{8}$
6. $1 \frac{3}{8}$
7. $1 \frac{1}{8}$
8. $1 \frac{1}{12}$
9. $\frac{7}{12}$
10. $\frac{11}{12}$
11. $1 \frac{1}{4}$
12. $1 \frac{1}{12}$
13. $\frac{7}{8}$
14. $\frac{5}{6}$
15. $1 \frac{1}{6}$

B.
1. $7 \frac{7}{8}$
2. $6 \frac{1}{3}$
3. $9 \frac{5}{8}$
4. $3 \frac{9}{20}$
5. $5 \frac{1}{2}$
6. $5 \frac{5}{8}$
7. $6 \frac{1}{9}$
8. 5
9. $8 \frac{7}{10}$
10. $10 \frac{3}{4}$
11. 5
12. $6 \frac{14}{15}$
13. $8 \frac{1}{4}$
14. $5 \frac{17}{20}$
15. $7 \frac{7}{8}$

PAGE 22

A.
1. $\frac{5}{8}$
2. $\frac{1}{6}$
3. $\frac{1}{6}$
4. $\frac{19}{30}$
5. $\frac{7}{20}$

Answers

PAGE 22 (continued)

6. $^1/_{12}$
7. $^2/_{15}$
8. $^1/_{10}$
9. $^1/_{20}$
10. $^2/_{21}$
11. $^1/_6$
12. $^1/_4$
13. $^4/_9$
14. $^3/_8$
15. $^2/_{15}$

B.
1. $3\,^1/_4$
2. $1\,^1/_8$
3. $4\,^1/_8$
4. $1\,^1/_8$
5. 2
6. $1\,^5/_8$
7. $4\,^1/_2$
8. $3\,^1/_2$
9. $2\,^1/_3$
10. $1\,^5/_{14}$
11. $1\,^1/_{20}$
12. $3\,^7/_{20}$
13. $1\,^2/_9$
14. $2\,^4/_{15}$
15. $3\,^5/_8$

PAGE 23

A.
1. 3,616
2. 1,159
3. 3,149
4. 4,537
5. 1,525
6. 7,429
7. 1,459
8. 1,799
9. 2,099

B.
1. 5,360
2. 1,484
3. 2,852
4. 3,997
5. 4,768
6. 4,397
7. 3,883

8. 2,942
9. 3,983

C.
1. 1,679
2. 1,386
3. 757
4. 7,788
5. 2,763
6. 1,834
7. 226
8. 4,965
9. 2,767

D.
1. 541
2. 5,285
3. 3,583
4. 4,682
5. 5,213
6. 6,334
7. 1,148
8. 266
9. 5,214

PAGE 24

A.
1. $^1/_5$
2. $1\,^3/_4$
3. $^1/_3$
4. $^1/_4$
5. 2
6. $^3/_8$
7. $^1/_8$
8. $1\,^2/_3$
9. $^1/_2$
10. $^9/_{80}$
11. $^1/_6$
12. $3\,^1/_3$
13. $^8/_{25}$
14. $^3/_{25}$
15. $^1/_8$

B.
1. $^4/_5$
2. $^3/_4$
3. 1
4. $3\,^3/_4$
5. 3
6. $^1/_2$

7. 2
8. 1
9. 2
10. $^1/_4$
11. $^3/_4$
12. $14\,^1/_2$
13. 6
14. 2
15. $1\,^1/_3$

PAGE 25

A.
1. $2\,^4/_5$
2. $1\,^1/_3$
3. $1\,^1/_2$
4. $1\,^1/_2$
5. 4
6. $^2/_3$
7. $^5/_6$
8. 2
9. $1\,^1/_3$
10. $1\,^1/_4$
11. 2
12. $1\,^1/_5$
13. $1\,^1/_3$
14. $2\,^2/_5$
15. $2\,^4/_5$

B.
1. $1\,^1/_2$
2. $^1/_6$
3. 2
4. $3\,^1/_2$
5. 12
6. 2
7. $2\,^2/_3$
8. 14
9. $^2/_3$
10. 6
11. $^3/_4$
12. 5
13. $^5/_6$
14. 12
15. $1\,^1/_2$

PAGE 26

A.
1. 176.34

2. 62.31
3. 110.99
4. 112.92
5. 61.17
6. 145.90
7. 114.07
8. 91.70
9. 129.97
10. 117.82
11. 129.96
12. 140.03
13. 81.89
14. 100.15
15. 48.78
16. 89.11
17. 99.88
18. 165.65
19. 144.89
20. 137

B.
1. 93.96
2. 254.30
3. 274.7
4. 208.46
5. 553.73
6. 1,002.8
7. 1,068.15
8. 618.79

PAGE 27

A.
1. 16.8
2. 45.79
3. 47.77
4. 35.03
5. 68.42
6. 15.91
7. 16.84
8. 345.51
9. 77.5
10. 60.28
11. 624.3
12. 28.33
13. 1.63

Answers

PAGE 27 (continued)

14. 2.57
15. 47.64
16. 45.70
17. 32.32
18. 71.67

B.

1. 62.87
2. 259.47
3. 0.87
4. 17.27
5. 27.63
6. 258.22
7. 18.61
8. 2.93
9. 61.24

PAGE 28

A.

1. 49,005
2. 17,620
3. 19,180
4. 20,300
5. 16,852
6. 31,815
7. 43,855
8. 25,120
9. 11,795

B.

1. 57,876
2. 22,365
3. 53,600
4. 13,534
5. 55,578
6. 23,001
7. 54,063
8. 34,830
9. 37,394

C.

1. 9,968
2. 18,196
3. 51,832
4. 80,001
5. 43,088
6. 13,275
7. 44,500
8. 72,918
9. 71,664

D.

1. 14,102
2. 5,184
3. 33,156
4. 17,246
5. 22,092
6. 25,680
7. 40,005
8. 12,481
9. 27,580

PAGE 29

1. 2 ,224.8
2. 1.7325
3. 37.252
4. 272.72
5. 82.94
6. 19.987
7. 15.861
8. 51.012
9. 1,144.6
10. 2.3004
11. 3,788.4
12. 0.2244
13. 1.0564
14. 2.7262
15. 491.12
16. 904.4
17. 26.159
18. 4.7658
19. 6,148.8
20. 190.44
21. 3,595.2
22. 1.4336
23. 0.10016
24. 24.893
25. 486.2
26. 190.4
27. 390.6
28. 28.251
29. 162.86

30. 3.69
31. 0.21982
32. 268.65
33. 65.749312
34. 3.925
35. 1,319.5
36. 3.336

PAGE 30

A.

1. 0.245
2. 4.87
3. 0.0371
4. 0.0035
5. 0.0002
6. 0.783
7. 0.0034
8. 0.22008

B.

1. 31.8
2. 0.146
3. 0.21
4. 1.18
5. 2.38
6. 0.118
7. 10.2
8. 0.106

C.

1. 4.6
2. 1.7
3. 13
4. 25
5. 3.7
6. 430
7. 21
8. 0.26
9. 0.32
10. 2.8

PAGE 31

A.

1. 1,432
2. 2,000
3. 800
4. 1,025
5. 1,481
6. 923

7. 1,437
8. 2,466
9. 1,512

B.

1. 1,350
2. 1,390
3. 1,500
4. 797
5. 1,157
6. 1,524
7. 408
8. 1,409
9. 651

C.

1. 1,065
2. 1,054
3. 625
4. 1,000
5. 408
6. 206
7. 337
8. 784
9. 1,197

D.

1. 1,650
2. 1,122
3. 1,078
4. 1,530
5. 2,553
6. 664
7. 582
8. 812
9. 2,084

PAGE 32

1. 112 g
2. 15.7
3. 261
4. 41
5. 41
6. 37 years
7. 137 months
8. 50 g
9. 60
10. 24 km
11. 708
12. 730 liters

Answers

PAGE 33

1. 4 kg
2. 54 times
3. 360
4. 15 m 5 cm
5. $131.60
6. 2 m 46 cm 3 mm
7. $10.26
8. $73.35
9. (a) $15.00
   (b) $1.50
10. 144
11. 24
12. $^1/_8$

PAGE 34

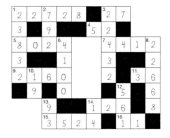

PAGE 35

Teacher check

PAGE 36

1. $^1/_2$
2. $^1/_{13}$
3. $^1/_4$
4. $^1/_{26}$
5. $^1/_{26}$
6. $^1/_{52}$
7. $^1/_{13}$
8. $^1/_4$
9. $^1/_{26}$
10. $^1/_{26}$
11. $^1/_2$
12. $^1/_{52}$
13. $^1/_{13}$
14. $^1/_{13}$
15. $^1/_4$
16. $^1/_{13}$
17. $^1/_4$
18. $^1/_{26}$

PAGE 37

1. 23:20
2. Jane 10 yrs 7 mths
   Paul 8 yrs 4 mths
3. 39 days
4. 12/21/1985
5. 145 hours
6. 3 hrs 13 mins
7. 20:50
8. 35 hours
9. 6 hrs 30 mins
10. 6 hours

PAGE 38

A.

1. 12:46 p.m.
2. 5:23 a.m.
3. 10:47 p.m.
4. 2:01 a.m.
5. 8:06 a.m.
6. 11:34 a.m.
7. 11:52 p.m.
8. 6:31 p.m.

B.

1. 0557
2. 1559
3. 1203
4. 2247
5. 1103
6. 0110
7. 1523
8. 2107

C.

1. 74 mins
2. 59 mins
3. 132 mins
4. 178 mins
5. 74 mins
6. 103 mins
7. 142 mins
8. 108 mins

PAGE 39

A.

A = 82.5 cm³
B = 90 cm³
C = 52.5 cm³
D = 96 cm³
E = 33 cm³
F = 120 cm³
G = 72 cm³
H = 115.5 cm³
I = 48 cm³
J = 67.5 cm³

B.

1. 210 cm³
2. 1 039.5 cm³
3. 495 cm³
4. 472.5 cm³
5. 360 cm³
6. 768 cm³

PAGE 40

A.

1. 8 L 248 ml
   or 8.248 L
2. 8 L 957 ml
   or 8.957 L
3. 9 L 176 ml
   or 9.176 L
4. 6 L 427 ml
   or 6.427 L
5. 0 L 520 ml
   or 0.520 L
6. 9 L 082 ml
   or 9.082 L
7. 3 L 353 ml
   or 3.353 L

B.

1. 7 L 638 ml
   or 7.638 L
2. 2 L 326 ml
   or 2.326 L
3. 34 L 068 ml
   or 34.068 L
4. 2 L 343 ml
   or 2.343 L
5. 24 L 168 ml
   or 24.168L

PAGE 41

1. 11 L 250 ml
2. 30 L
3. 3.254 L
4. 5 L 525 ml
5. (a) 60 L
   (b) 12 L
   (c) 84 L
   (d) 36 L
6. 2.2 L
7. 3 714 cm³
8. 13 days
9. 15.625 m³

PAGE 42

17 kg 623 g	✔	17.623 kg
15 kg 381 g	✔	15.381 kg
69 kg 385 g	79 kg 458 g	79.458 kg
3 kg 543 g	3 kg 543 g	3.543 kg
14 t 884 kg	14 t 884 kg	14.884 t
41 kg 810 g	✔	15.810 kg
41 t 155 kg	42 t 175 kg	42.175 t
3 t 898 kg	3 t 898 kg	3.898 t
29 t 330 kg	29 t 330 kg	29.330 t
6 t 628 kg	6 t 628 kg	6.628 t
6 kg 92 g	✔	6.091 kg
5 t 399 kg	5 t 399 kg	5.399 t
4 t 690 kg	4 t 609 kg	4.609 t
93 t 672 kg	93 t 672 kg	93.672 t

PAGE 43

1. 50 brackets
2. 1 kg 40 g
3. 25 boxes
4. 9 kg
5. 364 g
6. (a) 642 g
   (b) 963 g
   (c) 856 g
   (d) 856 g
   (e) 535 g
   (f) 428 g
7. (a) 2 kg 575 g
   (b) A and D